Swansea
scenes
and Suburbs

First published in Great Britain in 2009 by
Bryngold Books Ltd.,
Golden Oaks, 98 Brynau Wood, Cimla,
Neath, South Wales, SA11 3YQ.
www.bryngoldbooks.com

Typesetting, layout and design
by Bryngold Books

ISBN 978-1-905900-13-8

**Printed in Wales by
Gomer Press
Llandysul, Ceredigion.**

At the height of their popularity, sending postcards was as popular as text messaging is today. They were a quick and easy method of keeping in touch with friends and relatives wherever they were.

Early postcards though, had one advantage over their modern day, hi-tech counterparts — they survived to tell the tale! Better still, countless cards play a special role in reminding us of the way a particular place once was and thus play their own special part in recording history. Down the years postcards have served many other purposes too, not least helping to put a smile on our faces. Swansea Scenes and Suburbs may well do the same as it offers a second peep at at the collection of Alan Jones, a man who harbours a passion for collecting images of the way its proud people and places once were. They show many sides of city life — the serious and the not so. On the pages that follow there are many fresh and fascinating city street scenes but most importantly the book takes the reader on a journey through the sprawling suburbs that mushroomed as Swanseas's prosperity grew. Most districts are featured, along with a cheeky selection of the comedy cards.

The images are not arranged in any historical or time-based sequence, but simply a magical miscellany for the browser to savour at their leisure. Swansea Scenes and Suburbs is an unique look back in time at Wales finest seaside city in all its guises.

About the author

An avid collector of postcards Alan Jones was born and bred in Swansea and was a pupil of the city's Brynmill and Dynevor schools. His working life saw service in Swansea Council's treasurers department, the NCB, and finally Lloyds Bank, Morriston. Currently living in Sketty he and his wife Vivia have three children and five grandchildren.

A keen sportsman, Alan played at Junior Wimbledon in 1948 and has played a variety of other sports locally. For more than 30 years he was treasurer of Tennis Wales South and a councillor of Tennis Wales, becoming president between 2005-2007.

In nearly four decades of collecting postcards he has amassed a wide and varied collection which focuses mainly on Swansea. This book is the second to be born of his desire to share with others just a small selection of his more interesting finds.

Thanks

Thanks for their valued assistance in the compilation of this book are due in no small measure to David Roberts, Gerald Gabb, Swansea Museum, Byron Morris, Peter Muxworthy, Neville Browning, staff at the West Glamorgan Archive Service and Paul Reynolds.

Dedication

Swansea Scenes and Suburbs is dedicated to Brittany, Meghan, Sam, Joe and Amira.

An air of excitement would surely have filled this crowd of youngsters when a photographer turned up at the tram terminus in High Street, one day in 1904.

Upper High Street, 1915. Boots the Chemist had a strong presence then, near the station, on the right.

Castle Street as it appeared in the 1930s. The famous Kardomah cafe, popular with poet Dylan Thomas and his contemporaries, is in the centre.

Piering into the past! Here the majestic sweep of Swansea pier, stretches seawards into the distance behind a group of people out for a Sunday stroll, 1904. Meanwhile, in another early view of Swansea Pier, top left, a woman dressed in the fashion finery of the day appears to be posing for the cameraman. Bottom left: a vessel lies at anchor in the River Tawe in this view of the east and west piers and harbour, 1906. Kilvey Hill is in the background.

The Swan Hotel, Gower Street, early 1900s. In front of it can be seen the grounds of Mount Pleasant Chapel. The hotel failed to survive the ravages of the Second World War, but the chapel lives on.

Passengers leave a tram outside the Bay View Hotel at St Helen's. They were probably heading for a stroll along the prom or perhaps the nearby Mumbles Railway and a trip to the pier.

Being beside the seaside and beside the sea was an altogether different affair in 1905 as this picture of a group of children heading for a paddle testifies. No bikinis or bathers then — just the odd bare leg or two!

Goff and Edna Jones standing in the garden of 17 Clarence Terrace in 1929. If they stood there now they would be run over by the traffic in West Way between Clarence Terrace and Oxford Street.

Hospital Square looking up Brynymor Road, in 1907. The Westbourne Hotel occupies a commanding corner spot.

Vessels in the River Tawe near the entrance to the South Dock basin, early 1900s. Sail was still much in evidence though the tugs were powered by steam.

Swansea Hospital Convalescent Home, overlooking Cwmdonkin Park. Opened on July 17, 1903 most of its building cost had been paid by Miss Clara Thomas of Llwynmadoc. Amy Dillwyn was the motivating force behind the scheme.

A glimpse into the dining room of Swansea Hospital's convalescent home, Cwmdonkin.

A rare 1915 postcard of Richardson Street looking towards the new Drill Hall.

Castle Street in the early 1920s. The queue of men on the left may well have been waiting for the Labour Exchange to open.

How's this for a shop name? The Public Benefit Boot Company which stood on the corner of King Edward Road and Brynymor Road in 1914.

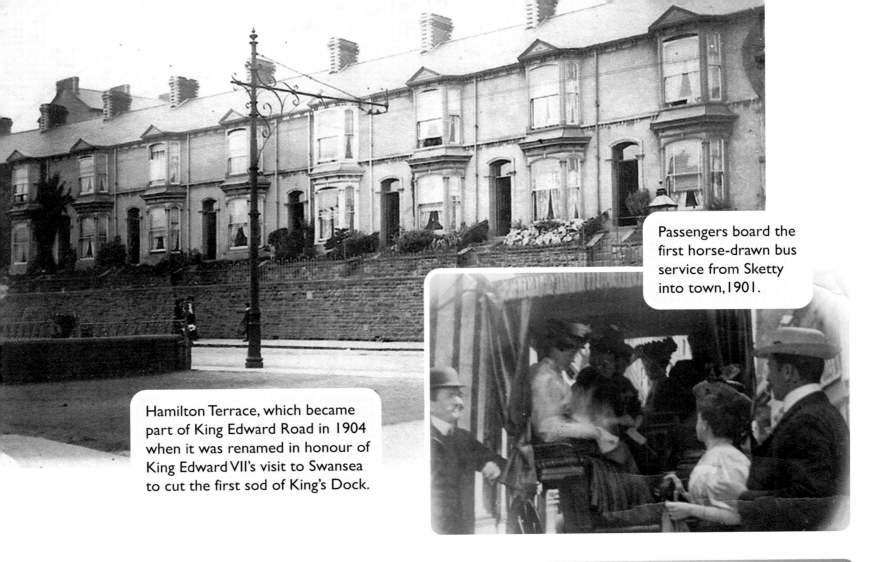

Passengers board the first horse-drawn bus service from Sketty into town, 1901.

Hamilton Terrace, which became part of King Edward Road in 1904 when it was renamed in honour of King Edward VII's visit to Swansea to cut the first sod of King's Dock.

The Spot newsagents on the corner of King Edward Road and Bay View Crescent, 1915.

The paved area in front of these shops in Uplands Crescent was originally the gardens of the properties alongside. They began life as houses, but one by one became popular retail outlets.

Mill Lane Blackpill, 1931.

The bus operated by Thomas Evans of Bryn Siriol Fforestfach on a route to Gorseinon.

Sketty Cross, early 1930s. Far less traffic meant there was no need for traffic lights then.

Western Street, Sketty, early 1900s.
Sketty Methodist Church is on the left.

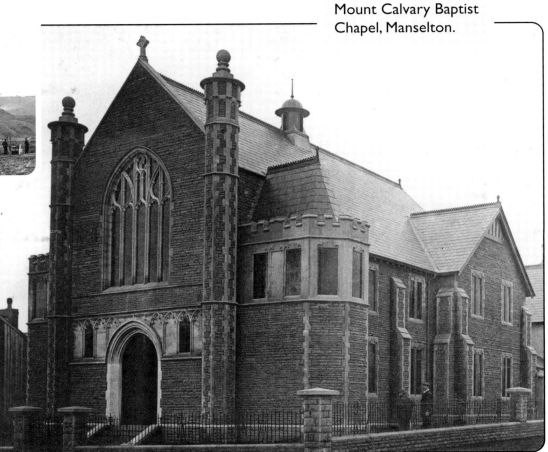

Mount Calvary Baptist Chapel, Manselton.

Manselton Congregational Church, 1908. Postcards were used like text messages in those days. On the back of this card is written: "My old woman thought I'd been to chapel so don't tell her different if you should meet her in the market on Saturday."

A view along Dyfed Avenue, Townhill, 1940s.

A mother and her young child stands with a group of youngsters in front of the Boer War memorial which stood at the entrance to Victoria Park.

Hendrefoilan House, Killay, 1904.

Llwynderw Hospital Annexe, West Cross. Dating from about 1830, it was briefly home to Ben Evans. In the 20th Century it became a hospital, then a convalescent home before being demolished in 1989 to make way for a housing development.

Looking towards West Cross, along Mumbles Road, Blackpill, 1922.

Glanmor was Swansea's first Central School for boys and girls. A stepping stone between elementary and secondary education, it opened on April 3, 1922. These pupils were members of the first girls intake. The school, top and bottom right, watched over by Swansea Training College, was previously a First World War American Army camp, hence the single storey wooden huts. During the Second World War the school was evacuated and the boys dispersed to Dynevor and Bishop Gore schools, but the girls returned until its eventual closure.

The pace of life was altogether slower in 1907 when this view of Birchgrove was captured on camera.

Some of the young residents of Birchgrove Road, Birchgrove, pose obligingly for the photographer, early 1920s.

Ravenhill Park, Fforestfach, certainly seems to have been a peaceful place to relax when this picture was taken.

An atmospheric winter's scene in Victoria Park.

An interesting view of Brynmill Park lake. The card suggests the lake offered fine boating in the heady days of 1903.

Staff of Llangyfelach station, 1923. It was on the Swansea District Line of the Great Western Railway. How useful would it be to have the chance to catch a train from there today, particularly for those who live locally.

The proud and upstanding members of the Llansamlet division of the St John Ambulance Brigade, June, 1912.

Looking along Woodfield Street, Morriston, towards St John's Church, 1910. The spire of Tabernacle Chapel can be seen stretching skywards on the left.

Looking up Crown Street, Morriston from Woodfield Street, 1905.

An industrial panorama of Morriston with the spire of Tabernacle Chapel vying with countless tinplate works chimneys for skywards supremacy, 1905.

The ornate structure in the centre of the roadway at Morriston Cross was a urinal. The Lamb and Flag pub is on the right, the Cross Inn on the left. Pentrepoeth Road can be seen snaking its way up from the centre.

The Baldwins United Women's football team with officials, 1920.

Cwmrhydyceirw Road, Morriston, looking towards its junction with Llanllienwen Road. Morriston Hospital had yet to be built when this scene was captured in 1905.

A more peaceful view of Landore, Graig Trewyddfa and Morris Castle. The castle as it is referred to was built as a tenement block for workers, one of the first of its kind.

Imposing Ynystawe House, summer 1906.

The bandstand at Cwmdonkin Park.

Saloam Baptist Chapel, Killay, 1912.

Brynhyfryd School, with some of its pupils playing in the roadway outside the entrance, something that would be unthinkable with today's volume of traffic there.

Llangyfelach Road at
Brynhyfryd Cross, 1927.

Some of the participants in a tennis competition at Langland, 1948. The man with the megaphone is Bruce Barter who stated the tournament in 1944.

One of the floats which took part in an early Swansea carnival.

The festive flair of the Ben Evans department store was boundless. This Christmastime float was designed to promote the arrival of Santa at the store. It must have been more comfortable for him than a reindeer-hauled sleigh.

EXPRESS DELIVERY

ALL TOYS
PURCHASED AT MESSRS.
BEN EVANS & Co's BAZAAR
WILL BE
DELIVERED PERSONALLY
BY
FATHER CHRISTMAS

Ben Evans & Co
SWANSEA
TEL. 1015.

Tirdeunaw, 1908, with Caersalem Chapel in the centre background. The obligatory people obliging the photographer by populating the view.

This road in Tirdeunaw appears as a haven of peace in 1936. Now it is a busy traffic route.

Caersalem graveyard, Tirdeunaw, 1905. The road to Caemawr and eventually Morriston can be seen on the top left

A group of earnest pupils at Llangyfelach School, 1909.

St Gabriel's Church,
Bryn Road, 1908.

Hats were the fashion accessory of the day for many of the men and women in this group photograph of Swansea summer school, 1910.

The soccer team of Lloyds Bank, Swansea, 1912. They won the Inter-bank Cup that year.

Dunvant, 1916. The wagons carried coal from a number of local collieries.

Killay railway station, 1906. This section of track opened as the Llanelly Railway in 1866.

Dunvant railway station, 1907.

The recreation ground, Mumbles Road, 1911.

Brynmill Park 1910.

A quiet corner of Brynmill Park, one of the many popular green oases that Swansea still boasts today.

Brynmill School, 1906. The author attended in later years and passed his 11-plus there in 1940!

Dear.............................. I HAVE ARRIVED AT SWANSEA.

Crowds follow behind a tank as it trundles through Swansea's streets helping to raise funds for the war effort in the 1914-18 conflict.

One of the first road accidents in Swansea. The charabanc had tried to squeeze past this car in Clasemont Road, Morriston, but without success, late 1920s.

The lane that became Derwen Fawr Road before it was widened and built along.

Derwen Fawr Road, Sketty, 1936. On the right hand side houses up to number 36 had been completed.

The start of building at Derwen Fawr Road, Sketty, early 1930s.

St Helen's Crescent in the 1920s, before the Guildhall was built. The entrance to Victoria Park was on the left.

Ben Evans Christmas festivities. This was at Mumbles Road end of Singleton Park and shows its fairy grotto. The message on the back of the card read: "Father Christmas has now arrived and extends to you a hearty invitation to come and see the fairy house, Felix and jumbo at the bazaar.

Clydach Road, Llansamlet
and inset: the Uplands, 1909.

Visitors listen to a speaker at the Royal National Eisteddfod of Wales, Singleton Park, August, 1907.

They don't make them like this anymore! This vehicle would certainly have carried its owner into town in style in the early 1900s. It is parked in the grounds of a house that still stands alongside Mumbles Road, West Cross.

The Winter Gardens and lounge of the Metropole Hotel, Wind Street.

King Edward Road, looking towards St Helen's, 1910.

Passengers on the Mumbles Train head back to Swansea as a group of cyclists pass them in the opposite direction. The Recreation ground and St Helen's sports ground are on the left.

.. CORONATION OF GEORGE V. ...

Sketty Festivities.

THE CHAIRMAN AND COMMITTEE
request the pleasure of

M*rs* *Thos. Williams*

Company at DINNER, on Thursday, June 22nd,
at the Church Hall, Sketty, at 7 p.m.

Please reply to either—
R. F. BROWNE, } Hon.
T. MORRIS, } Secretaries.

An invitation card to a dinner which was part of festivities held at Sketty to mark the Coronation of King George V at the church hall, June 22, 1937.

A group of students at Swansea Wireless Training College, 1918.

A view of the magnificent flower beds in Victoria Park, 1916.

Gwydr Crescent, Uplands, 1907.

These houses in Pantygwydr Road have changed little since this 1917 view was captured.

The Trinity Choir leaving in a charabanc from outside the old town Labour exchange and Post Office, Morriston, on an outing to Pontneathvaughan, in the Neath Valley, 1923.

The Wesley Chapel AFC, Glantawe Street, Morriston, 1926-1927.

The view from Pantycelyn Road, Townhill, 1927. Rosehill tennis courts can be seen on the bottom left.

Looking towards Townhill from Walter Road.

With the exception of a woman giving birth and the midwife attending her, this is a very early 1900s photograph taken at a gathering of all of Sketty's villagers.

Tycoch Road, Sketty, looking deserted in 1911.

Clydach Road showing the primitive Methodist Chapel building and to the left in the background, Pentrepoeth School.

Clydach Council Schools Ynystawe, now Ynystawe Primary School.

Countless works and factory chimneys pump out smoke and steam over Landore, 1910.

A panoramic view of Landore, 1910. It clearly shows how industrial the area was at this time.

Swansea's other Ben Evans.
This one ran a fish and
chip shop in Morriston!

The GJ Bourne, Furnishing House,
Fabian Street, St Thomas, 1907.

The Morriston United Quoit Club which, judging by the number of its members was a thriving one.

Family and friends of Morriston dentist Mr Nicholls at High Street Station, sending him on the first leg of his journey of emigration to Australia, 1924.